DANCE

Ballet
Dance

by Karen Marie Graves

Consultant:
Nicole LaFleur Amadeo, Education Director
American Repertory Ballet

Capstone
press®

Mankato, Minnesota

Snap Books are published by Capstone Press,
151 Good Counsel Drive, P.O. Box 669, Mankato, Minnesota 56002.
www.capstonepress.com

Library of Congress Cataloging-in-Publication Data

Graves, Karen Marie.
Ballet dance / by Karen Marie Graves.
    p. cm.—(Snap books. Dance)
    Summary: "Describes ballet dancing, including history, training, moves,
and performance"—Provided by publisher.
    Includes bibliographical references and index.
    ISBN-13: 978-1-4296-0119-1 (hardcover)
    ISBN-10: 1-4296-0119-1 (hardcover)
    1. Ballet—Juvenile literature. 2. Ballet dancing—Juvenile literature.
3. Ballet. 4. Ballet dancing. I. Title. II. Series.
GV1787.5.G726 2008
792.8—dc22   2007005397

Editor: Megan Schoeneberger

Designer: Veronica Bianchini

Photo Researchers: Laura Manthe and Wanda Winch

Photo Credits:
Capstone Press/Karon Dubke, cover, 2–3, 8, 9, 10, 11, 12, 13, 14 (both), 15, 16 (both), 17 (all), 18, 19, 20, 21, 22, 23, 24,
25; Christopher Jean-Richard/Dancers Daniela Buson and Alfonso Martin in Tulsa Ballet's Swan Lake, 7; Columbia
Artists Management Inc., 26–27; Corbis/Kevin Fleming, 29; courtesy of author Karen Graves, 32; Getty Images Inc./
AFP, 4–5; Marty Sohl, 27; Shutterstock/Matt Ellis, 22, 23, 24, 25; Wikipedia, public-domain, 6

Capstone Press thanks Annmarie and the students of the Mankato Ballet Company, Mankato, Minnesota.

1 2 3 4 5 6 12 11 10 09 08 07

Table of Contents

An Athlete in Disguise

The music swells, and the ballerina launches into spin after spin of dizzying turns.

She leaps, holding her head high and stretching her arms to the sky. For a moment, she floats. Her tutu catches the air like a falling snowflake.

A ballet dancer may look as light as a bird, but don't be fooled.

There's steel beneath that tutu. In addition to dance classes, dancers do a demanding program of strength, cardiovascular, and flexibility training. A ballet dancer is an artist and an athlete.

"To dance is to be out of yourself. Larger, more beautiful, more powerful. This is power, it is glory on earth and it is yours for the taking."

Agnes de Mille, dancer and choreographer

Ballet Beginnings

Ballet is a dance that tells a story through movement and music.

It began in the 1400s as a way to entertain royalty at elegant parties in the palaces of Italy and France. King Louis XIV of France started the first ballet school in 1661.

In the 1800s, fairies, spirits, and other supernatural beings became popular ballet subjects. During this time, women began dancing on their toes, or sur les pointes, to suggest floating or flying. Toe dancing remains one of the most recognizable characteristics of ballet today.

Swan Lake, 1901

Many early ballets, like *The Nutcracker* and *Swan Lake*, used music specifically written for the dance. In the early 1900s, choreographers started using other classical music. Choreographers experimented with rock 'n' roll and jazz music in the 1960s.

Ballet Today

Swan Lake, 2003

Ballet may be classic, but it's not stuck in the past.

After years of influencing other dance forms, ballet has begun taking something in return. Now, ballet programs include restagings of older ballets as well as presentations of new forms and interpretations. Some of today's creative ballets include hip-hop, bluegrass, or whatever strikes the choreographer's chord!

Chapter Two

Ballet Basics

This book will give you a pretty good idea of what ballet is all about.

But any dancer will tell you that you can't really learn ballet from a book or DVD. Ballet is very technical. Doing moves incorrectly can lead to bad habits or, even worse, injury. You don't want to end your ballet career before you begin, so you'll need a good teacher.

You can prepare yourself for ballet before you even step on a dance floor. Ballet dancers need strength, stamina, and flexibility. Try running, swimming, biking, or jumping rope to build up your strength and stamina. Yoga or pilates will increase your flexibility.

Welcome to the Studio

Ballet is usually taught in studios designed for ballet dancers. The studio should have plenty of open space. Large mirrors on the wall allow the dancers to check their technique. There should also be handrails called barres to help dancers keep their balance. Barres can be attached to a wall or freestanding.

To Tutu or Not to Tutu

For class, you won't need a tutu. Instead, you'll need a leotard and tights. They'll allow a teacher to clearly see your body position and alignment.

For footwear, you'll need a pair of simple, soft leather ballet slippers. Don't run out and buy a pair of toe shoes yet. Ballerinas wear these satin slippers for toe dancing. It takes years to build up the strength to dance on your toes.

Keep your hair simple and neat. If you have long hair, twist it into a bun. Short hair should be pinned back away from your face.

Tip!

Before you buy anything, check with the studio. Some studios require certain colors of clothing and shoes.

11

Taking the First Leap

You found a studio, signed up for class, and got the gear. You're ready to go. What can you expect next?

A ballet class usually begins at the barre with exercises to warm up and stretch. The second part of a class, called center work, is in the center of the floor. It often starts with slow exercises to help with balance. As class goes on, the pace quickens. Dancers move across the floor with jumps, turns, and traveling steps. At the very end of class, dancers return to center floor. They perform a brief bow to thank their teacher for the class.

Turnout and Posture

All ballet positions require turnout. Turnout means the legs are rotated outward, starting from the hip. With proper turnout, the entire leg, knee, and foot face sideways. You probably won't be able to turn out fully at first. It will come in time as your body becomes more flexible.

Good posture, or line, is as important to ballet as it is to your parents. It makes a dancer appear longer and more graceful. For good posture, imagine a straight line from the top of your head through the center of your body to the floor. Stand tall with your back straight. Now pull in your stomach, relax your shoulders, and lengthen your neck. Hold your head straight with your chin level.

Get in Position

Everything you do in ballet starts from a few basic arm and foot positions. You'll work on them in beginning classes and keep working on them as you advance. It takes a lot of time and effort to do them right. Even professional ballet dancers practice the basic positions every day.

Positions of the Arms and Feet

All movements start, pass through, and end with five basic positions. It's important to get them right from the beginning. Remember your turnout. Your knees should always point in the same direction as your toes. As you practice, keep your arms softly bent. Movements should start from the shoulders, not the elbows.

First

Hold your arms in an oval in front of your body, as though you're holding a large beach ball.

Put your heels together, making a "V" with your feet.

Second

Open your arms to the side, rounding them slightly.

Stand in first position, but with your feet apart.

Third

From second position, bring one arm up so your palm faces your forehead.

Place the heel of one foot at the instep of the other.

Fourth

Bring the other arm to the front like it was in first position.

Bring the foot at your instep forward.

Fifth

From fourth position, bring the front arm up, making an oval a little in front of your head. Both palms face your forehead.

The heel in the front foot is against the big toe in the opposite foot.

Once you learn the basic foot and arm positions, you'll start with some simple barre exercises.

Demi Plié

First you will learn the demi plié. Starting with your feet in first position, bend your knees about halfway down. Make sure your knees stay in line with your toes, and press your heels into the floor.

Barre

Relevé

Starting with your feet in first position, gradually lift both heels off the floor at the same time. Keep your knees straight and your weight over the balls of your feet.

Chapter Four

Raising the Barre

After you learn the basic moves and positions, you're well on your way to becoming a ballet dancer.

Advanced ballet classes are based on beginning classes. You'll do more difficult versions of the exercises and steps you know. You also may take specialized classes. In pas de deux class you'll learn how to dance with a partner. In variations class, you'll learn parts from famous ballets.

What's the Pointe?

Your instructor will decide when your legs and feet are strong enough to dance on pointe. At first, you'll do some exercises at the end of class to learn the basics and build up strength. Then you can take a pointe class devoted only to dancing on your tiptoes.

Most girls never forget the thrill of owning their first pair of toe shoes. The toes in these satin slippers are strengthened with layers of glue and burlap. But even with the extra strength, toe shoes wear out quickly. Most professional ballet dancers use about 10 pairs of toe shoes a month. A soloist, or principal dancer, uses about 20. She often goes through three or four different pairs for one performance!

Center Work

As you improve, what kind of positions and steps can you expect to learn? Three common moves are arabesques, pirouettes, and jetés.

Arabesque

For an arabesque, the dancer stands on one leg and extends the other behind her. The arms can be held in many different positions.

Pirouette

A pirouette is an advanced turn. The dancer spins on one leg with the other leg in one of many positions.

Grand Jeté

Grand jetés are large leaps from one leg to the other. The legs are stretched out to look like the dancer is doing the splits in the air.

Following Your Dream

Of course you've dreamed of taking center stage as a prima ballerina.

Just about every girl has at some point in her life. To make the dream a reality, you'll need to be determined, stay focused, and of course, keep practicing.

Advanced students often take three to six ballet classes a week. Professional dancers take at least one class a day.

SPOTLIGHT:
Misty Copeland

It's never too late to follow your dreams, and Misty Copeland is proof. She had never even seen a ballet before she began her first ballet class at age 13. Six years and a lot of hard work later, Misty joined the American Ballet Theatre's corps de ballet.

Making It

For professional training, you can turn to private studios or to ballet schools. Many large ballet companies have their own schools. Ballet schools require auditions before you can enroll. Auditions are very competitive, so make sure you are ready.

Getting into a ballet company is even harder than getting into a ballet school. Dancers who make the cut usually start out in the corps de ballet. Later, if you're one of the very best, you could become a principal dancer.

Whether a soloist or a backup dancer, a professional dancer's life is pretty much all dance, all the time. In addition to daily classes, she usually has rehearsals—sometimes three or four a day. She has makeup, shoes, and costumes to take care of. Finally, she has the performance. Then it starts all over again the next day. It's hard but rewarding work. If you love ballet, your path to the spotlight can start today.

Glossary

alignment (uh-LINE-muhnt)—being in a straight line

barre (BAR)—the horizontal wooden bar used by dancers for support and balance

choreographer (kor-ee-OG-ruh-fur)—someone who arranges dance steps and movements for a ballet or show

corps de ballet (KOR duh bal-LAY)—the group of dancers who perform together as part of a ballet company

instep (IN-step)—the top part of your foot between your toes and your ankle

pas de deux (pah duh DOO)—a dance for two performers

Fast Facts

The first ballerina to dance on pointe was Marie Taglioni. In 1832, she performed in *La Sylphide*.

Ballerina Pierina Legnani is famous for performing 32 consecutive turns while dancing the part of Odette in *Swan Lake* in 1895.

The New York City Ballet's annual performance of *The Nutcracker* uses 150 costumes.

Read More

Castle, Kate. *The World of Ballet.* Boston: Kingfisher, 2005.

Dillman, Lisa. *Ballet.* Get Going! Hobbies. Chicago: Heinemann, 2006.

Schorer, Suki, and the School of American Ballet. *Put Your Best Foot Forward: A Young Dancer's Guide to Life.* New York: Workman, 2005.

Yolen, Jane, and Heidi E. Y. Stemple. *The Barefoot Book of Stories from the Ballet.* Cambridge, Mass.: Barefoot Books, 2004.

Internet Sites

FactHound offers a safe, fun way to find Internet sites related to this book. All of the sites on FactHound have been researched by our staff.

Here's how:

1. Visit *www.facthound.com*

2. Choose your grade level.

3. Type in this book ID **1429601191** for age-appropriate sites. You may also browse subjects by clicking on letters, or by clicking on pictures and words.

4. Click on the **Fetch It** button.

Facthound will fetch the best sites for you!

31

About the Author

Karen Marie Graves started ballet at 9 years old after receiving lessons as her all-time favorite birthday gift. While a student at the University of California, Los Angeles, she paid for her classes by teaching dance. After graduation, she continued teaching and began writing part time. She was Dance Director of the Children's Department at UCLA and taught ballet, tap, and jazz dance for 20 years before becoming a full-time writer.

INDEX